Sparks F Shadows

Chris Stubbs

India | USA | UK

Sparks From The Shadows © 2023 Chris Stubbs

All rights reserved.

No part of this publication may be reproduced, stored in a retrieval system, or transmitted, in any form or by any means, electronic, mechanical, photocopying, recording or otherwise, without the prior written permission of the presenters.

Chris Stubbs asserts the moral right to be identified as author of this work.

Presentation by *BookLeaf Publishing*

Web: www.bookleafpub.com

E-mail: info@bookleafpub.com

ISBN: 9789358319156

First edition 2023

"To the eternal dance of words and emotions, may 'Sparks from the Shadows' illuminate hearts and kindle the fires of imagination. With gratitude for the readers who dare to explore the realms of verse and find solace in the beauty of darkness."

ACKNOWLEDGEMENT

I would like to thank my amazing future wife Emma Shaw for constantly helping and supporting me.

And my Mum & Dad and my amazing son Connor for loving me as much as they do.

PREFACE

In the quiet recesses of our souls, hidden within the folds of our experiences, lie the sparks of illumination that defy the shadows that life casts. These are the sparks we often overlook, the flickers of light that emerge from the depths of our existence, even in the darkest of times. "Sparks from the Shadows" is a collection of verses that seeks to unearth these profound moments of radiance, hope, and understanding.

Within these pages, you will embark on a journey that navigates the labyrinth of human emotions. It is an exploration of love's warmth, the trials and triumphs of life, the relentless grip of anxiety, and the eternal dance between darkness and light. These verses are both an offering of vulnerability and a celebration of resilience, each poem an intimate conversation with the heart, inviting reflection and connection.

Through the art of poetry, we delve into the complexity of our shared human experiences. These words echo the whispers of our inner selves, beckoning us to recognize that within every shadow, there is a spark waiting to ignite. They encourage us to embrace the full spectrum of our emotions, to find strength in our vulnerability, and to kindle the flames of hope even when the world around us seems darkest.

As you journey through "Sparks from the Shadows," I invite you to embrace the fullness of your own existence, to reflect on the sparks that have illuminated your path, and to find solace in the understanding that, in the end, it is these very sparks that guide us through the labyrinth and lead us toward the light.

With gratitude and inspiration,

Chris Stubbs

Fluttering Love: A Butterfly Ballet

In meadows kissed by the golden sun's embrace,
Two butterflies met in a gentle, swirling chase.
With wings like painted dreams, they took to the air,
Dancing on the breeze, a love so rare.

Their colors, vibrant, a vivid display,
In the boundless sky, they found their way.
In a world of blossoms and skies so blue,
Their love blossomed, forever true.

In graceful spirals, they twirled and soared,
Their love story in the skies, adored.
Two butterflies, a love story from above,
Dancing, entwined, in a world of love.

Messages from Angels

In skies above, where dreams take flight,
Angel feathers softly gleam with light.
They drift from realms of grace and love,
A gift from heavens, sent from above.

In whispers of wind, they gently fall,
Bringing comfort to one and all.
Each feather holds a sacred grace,
A reminder of an angel's embrace.

In times of darkness, they appear,
Wiping away every doubt and fear.
A sign that angels are always near,
Their presence, a solace so sincere.

So cherish these feathers, pure and white,
Tokens of hope in the darkest night.
For in their delicate, ethereal grace,
Lies a glimpse of heaven's embrace.

Whispers of Restless Mind's

In shadows deep, anxiety does creep,
A silent storm, in restless sleep.
Its whispers haunt, both day and night,
A battle waged, out of sight.

Heart's frantic beat, a racing mind,
Invisible chains, hard to unwind.
But know, dear soul, you're not alone,
In this struggle, strength has grown.

Seek the light, embrace the day,
Anxiety's grip, it can decay.
With courage strong, you'll find your way,
Through darkest nights, to brighter day.

Guiding Glow in the Night's Embrace

In the depths of night so deep,
A flicker of hope, a light to keep.
Amid the shadows, it softly gleams,
Guiding us through our midnight dreams.

A beacon in the darkest hour,
Revealing paths with gentle power.
In its warm embrace, we find our way,
The light in darkness, night to day.

Autumn's Night Whispers

Beneath a moon's soft, silver glow,
Autumn nights in quiet flow,
Leaves of crimson, gold take flight,
Whispering secrets in the night.

Cool breeze dances through the trees,
Rustling secrets on the breeze,
Stars above, a sparkling sight,
In the stillness of autumn night.

Crackling fires, warm and bright,
Chase away the chill of night,
Cozy moments, hearts ignite,
In the embrace of autumn's night.

Rising Through Defeat

In the face of defeat, we find our might,
For in struggle's darkness, we discover light.
Though battles may be lost along the way,
They pave the path to a brighter day.

Defeat is but a teacher, stern and wise,
It humbles hearts and opens up the skies.
With courage and resolve, we rise anew,
To conquer challenges, old and new.

So embrace defeat as a stepping stone,
To strength and wisdom yet unknown.
For in each setback, a seed of success,
And in perseverance, we truly progress.

Smiles of Love: Illuminating Hearts

In a world of shadows, it shines so bright,
A loving smile, a pure delight.
With warmth in its curve and kindness in its glow,
It's a beacon of love wherever we go.

It speaks of joy and cares to share,
A silent language, beyond compare.
In moments of sadness, it brings us cheer,
A loving smile, forever dear.

So let us all, in our own unique style,
Share the gift of a loving smile.

Lost and Found: A Self-Rediscovery

Amidst the struggles and the strife,
I sought the path to a better life.
Through self-reflection, I began to see,
The person I was always meant to be.

With each step forward, I left behind,
The doubts and fears that once confined.
In the mirror's reflection, a newfound grace,
I found myself again, in a better place.

Embracing Pure Empathy

In hearts where empathy resides so pure,
We share the sorrows others must endure.
No judgment, just a listening, caring ear,
To understand the pain, to calm the fear.

With open hearts, we bridge the great divide,
In empathy, our compassion we confide.
For in the depths of feelings, we unite,
In pure empathy, we find the light.

Battling Inner Demons

In the shadows of our mind's dark domain,
Demons lurking, causing endless pain.
A battle fierce, a war we must begin,
To conquer inner demons, from deep within.

With courage as our sword and hope our shield,
We'll face the darkness that will not yield.
In this tumultuous struggle, we find our might,
To banish those demons and embrace the light.

Eclipsing Mistakes

Mistakes are but stepping stones in our past,
They do not define us, they will not last.
We learn, we grow, we rise above,
In the light of our potential, we find our love.

A canvas of life, with colors so vast,
Mistakes are just moments, they're not meant to last.
For we are the artists of our destiny's art,
Not bound by errors, but by the strength in our heart.

Eternal Love's Discovery

Amid the crowd, a face so true,
My heart recognized, it had found you.
In your eyes, a world I dream of,
You are my one true love.

Hand in hand, through life we'll roam,
Together, we've found our cherished home.
In your arms, my heart takes flight like a dove,
Forever, you are my one true love.

Casting Out Anxiety's Shadow

In shadows deep, anxiety may rise,
But in our hearts, a spark, a light defies.
With courage strong, we face the daunting day,
Not letting anxious whispers lead us astray.

In every breath, we find our steady ground,
With hope and strength, a refuge can be found.
Though anxious winds may howl and try to sway,
We stand resilient, fear cannot hold sway.

For in our hearts, we'll conquer and begin,
To let the strength within our souls outspin.
Anxiety may knock, but we won't let it in,
In the face of fear, we're bound to win.

Concealed Emotions

A smile, so bright, can secrets keep,
Behind those lips, emotions deep.
It hides the tears, the inner strife,
Concealing battles, hidden life.

In joy it dances, but in disguise,
A smile can mask the sorrow's guise.
Beneath the grins, the world unknown,
A heart's true story, seldom shown.

So when you see a smile so wide,
Remember, much may lie inside.
A world of feelings, tucked away,
Behind that smile, night and day.

Whispers of the Tides

Beneath the sky they break,
Crashing waves, a wild, untamed wake.
With every surge, a tale is told,
Of mysteries beneath, and treasures old.

In their tumultuous, relentless song,
They've journeyed far and wide, and long.
Yet in their chaos, a soothing grace,
A reminder of Earth's enduring embrace.

With each collision, they declare,
The power of nature, fierce and rare.
Crashing waves, a relentless art,
That etches its mark on every heart.

Melody of Raindrops

Raindrops fall with a gentle sound,
Nature's lullaby, soft on the ground.
A soothing rhythm, a calming refrain,
The song of rain, a peaceful domain.

Each drop a note in a watery symphony,
Dancing on leaves, a wondrous cacophony.
They whisper secrets to the earth below,
In their liquid song, a melody they bestow.

So close your eyes and listen well,
To the raindrops' tale they gently tell.
In their song, find solace and grace,
As they wash the world, in this quiet embrace.

Breaking Free from Anxiety's Chains

In the battlefield of my mind, I fought,
Anxiety's grip, relentless thought.
With courage as my shining shield,
I faced the darkness, would not yield.

Through therapy, I learned to cope,
Mindful breathing, gave me hope.
In time, I found the strength within,
To conquer fears, let new days begin.

Anxiety's shadow, once so tall,
I faced it down, broke down the wall.
With resilience, I took my stand,
And now, I hold my life in my hand.

Midnight Journey

Amidst the night, I take my ride,
In solitude, I find my guide.
The road ahead, a path unknown,
In serenity, my heart has grown.

The world asleep, the stars aglow,
The late-night drive, a tranquil flow.
Whispers of wind, a silent song,
In solitude, I truly belong.

With every turn, with every mile,
I find in darkness, a secret smile.
The serenity of this late-night drive,
In stillness, I come alive.

Whispers of the Heart

In the spaces where words don't dare,
A silent language fills the air.
Unspoken love, a bond so deep,
In quiet hearts, its secrets keep.

Eyes that meet and never part,
Convey the whispers of the heart.
A touch, a smile, a knowing glance,
In this silence, love's sweet dance.

No need for words, for love's embrace,
Speaks volumes with a gentle grace.
The silent language, pure and true,
In unspoken love, I find my cue.

Woodland Serenity

Hand in hand, we stroll through woods so green,
A peaceful world where nature's beauty's seen.
The whispering leaves and birds above,
In each other's company, we find our love.

Amongst the trees, we find our way,
Sharing dreams in the light of day.
With every step, our hearts align,
In the woods, our souls entwine.

The dappled sunlight, the forest's embrace,
With you, my love, it's a perfect place.
In the woods, our spirits find their song,
Walking together, where we belong.

Headway Wander

Beneath the open sky so wide,
I take a walk, with purpose, stride.
To clear my head, I roam alone,
With each step, a weight is thrown.

The worries fade, the mind's set free,
As I wander by land and sea.
A peaceful path to thoughts anew,
In this simple act, I renew.

The world outside, a gentle guide,
As I let go, I feel inside.
A walk to clear my head, you see,
Becomes a journey back to me.

Milton Keynes UK
Ingram Content Group UK Ltd.
UKHW050642150424
441175UK00014B/595